Original title:
Tails of the Trees

Copyright © 2025 Creative Arts Management OÜ
All rights reserved.

Author: Nathaniel Blackwood
ISBN HARDBACK: 978-1-80567-314-9
ISBN PAPERBACK: 978-1-80567-613-3

Dialogues in the Dancing Leaves

In the breeze, the branches sway,
Squirrels gossip all day long.
They chatter 'bout the sun's bright ray,
And hum a silly, cheerful song.

A raccoon rolls with a nut in hand,
He tumbles down, what a sight!
The trees all laugh, it's so unplanned,
As acorns take their cosmic flight.

A wise old owl gives a hoot,
'Watch where you step, you silly deer!'
The leaves join in with a giggly toot,
As critters dance without a fear.

'Why did the twig cross the trail?'
To join the ruckus, don't you see?
Together they laugh and tell a tale,
Of nature's joy and pure glee.

The Adventure of the Veil of Vines

Tangled among leaves in a funny twist,
A squirrel plots schemes that can't be missed.
He dangles and swings, oh what a sight,
In his leafy cradle, he feels just right.

Giggling at owls, all wise in the night,
He fashions a crown, snug and tight.
A merry parade down the branches so steep,
In his vine-woven palace, he dances to sleep.

History Etched in Roots and Rings

Beneath the bark, stories unwind,
Of acorns and twigs, and what you might find.
A raccoon in dusk, with a historian's flair,
Tales of the forest, light-hearted and rare.

Whispers of chaos from branches above,
As the beetles debate who they like, they shove.
In every knot, a laugh springs anew,
History's goofy, just look at the view!

The Auras of Arboreal Elders

Wisdom drips slowly from boughs overhead,
While chipmunks recite the tales that they've read.
With the rustle of leaves and a burst of delight,
The elders tell jokes as day turns to night.

Gnarled with laughter, their trunks start to sway,
As squirrels engage in a frolicsome play.
With branches like arms, they shimmy and shake,
Each chuckle a ripple, with each giggle, they quake.

Songs of Succulent Spectacle

A cactus belts high notes, a hilarious choir,
While the pompous palm poses like it's caught in fire.
With petals that twirl and a thistle who sings,
The garden erupts with the joy that it brings.

In the sunlight's embrace, and shadows they weave,
Flora join in, with giggles up their sleeve.
Each bloom has a story, in colors so bright,
Dancing on breezes, they chuckle in flight.

The Enchantment of Arborial Melodies

In the breeze, leaves giggle and sway,
Squirrels plotting their next hideaway.
Barking dogs join in the jest,
As branches dance, they're at their best.

Gnarled limbs twist in silly shapes,
Whispering secrets of ancient tapes.
Acorns bouncing, a playful game,
Nature's laughter, it's never tame.

Chronicles of the Forest Spirits

Under the twinkle of cheeky stars,
Mice wear hats, strumming guitars.
Bunnies hop, donning shades of green,
Forest spirits have quite a scene.

A raccoon juggles berries with flair,
While owls chuckle in their tall chair.
Every shadow plays a prank,
In this woodland, laughter's a rank.

The Grace of Gnarled Giants

Tall trunks twist like a dancer's spin,
With knots and curls, they pull you in.
Roots doing the cha-cha down below,
While squirrels giggle, putting on a show.

Branches bow for a forest ball,
With pinecones rolling, they trip and fall.
Even the moss knows how to groove,
These giant wonders really do move!

Symphony of Shadows in Shelters

Whispers of wind play a soft tune,
While critters gather beneath the moon.
A raccoon wears a leaf as a hat,
As shadows dance, they're wise to chat.

Chipmunks giggle in their burrowed beds,
Dropping acorns, soft on their heads.
In this ballet of nature's cheer,
Every rustle brings laughter near.

Enigmas Encased in Emerald

In the forest, a squirrel did prance,
With acorns gathered, he took a chance.
A raccoon danced, wearing a hat,
While a wise old owl said, "What of that?"

Frogs in a chorus sang funny tunes,
As the mushrooms swayed beneath the moons.
Shadows did giggle, colors did blend,
Nature's folly, where silliness trends.

The Temporal Trunk Tales

A tree spoke softly, its bark like wise,
Telling tales of squirrels in costumes that rise.
"Once we stole apples from Farmer McGee,
He shouted in vain, 'What's wrong with a bee?'"

The branches shook laughter, as if in delight,
With knots in the trunk that giggled at night.
A fox wore spectacles, read stories aloud,
While the winds blew in chuckles, gathering a crowd.

Revelry in the Realm of Roots

Deep underground, the critters would meet,
Roots tangled in laughter, a curious feat.
Worms held a party, cool shades in the dirt,
While ants wore tuxedos, and loved their dessert.

Ladybugs twirled in a grand little dance,
While daisies helped frogs host a leaf-laden "prance."
A party with laughter across all the land,
Nature's own jester with a green, leafy band.

Flourish of Fables in Flora

In the meadow, the daisies did boast,
Of tales from the wind, they loved the most.
A bee in a bonnet served tea on the grass,
While butterflies giggled as they watched the class.

The oak told a story of being quite tall,
Proud of its branches and leaves that enthrall.
Its shadow cast laughter, beneath sunny rays,
In the garden of giggles, where time always plays.

Harmonies of the Highboughs

Swaying branches have a tune,
They sing beneath the smiling moon.
Acorns drop like little drums,
While squirrels dance to summon crumbs.

Rustling leaves make whispered jokes,
As chipmunks join in with their pokes.
The winds laugh as they spin and twirl,
Nature's choir in a leafy whirl.

Echoed Leaves of Enchantment

Leaves converse in silly rhymes,
Whispering secrets over times.
One leaf says, 'I am the best!'
Another flutters, 'I'm quite blessed!'

A breeze winks like a playful friend,
As branches twist and try to bend.
Expecting rain, they humorously pout,
While birds add laughter, chirping about.

The Dance of Branches in Bloom

In springtime's dance, the branches prance,
They wiggle and jiggle, a curious stance.
Blossoms giggle, dressed in bright hues,
As bugs do the cha-cha, shaking their shoes.

Great oaks tease younger saplings near,
'You're not tall enough! Better steer clear!'
Yet all in jest, the forest's a stage,
With laughter echoing, ageless and sage.

Nature's Canvas of Canopies

Above, the leaves paint a wild scene,
With colors that spark joy, vivid and green.
A painter squirrel with a brush in hand,
Adds splashes of fun across the land.

The tree trunks chuckle, sturdy and wise,
They share stories below the bright skies.
Carved hearts and initials bolster the cheer,
Nature's own art, valued and dear.

Whispers of Whimsy in Woodlands

In the woods where critters dance,
Squirrels hold a nutty romance.
Branches sway with giggly glee,
Chatting tales of what could be.

Rabbits wear their hats askew,
While the owls hoot a tune or two.
Blades of grass laugh in the breeze,
Softly rustling like chuckled leaves.

A raccoon juggles shiny rocks,
While tree trunks laugh in silly knocks.
Do you hear the whispers loud?
Nature's antics make us proud!

The Lullaby of Leafy Legacy

Boughs sway softly, singing sweet,
A lullaby for tiny feet.
In the canopy, a party wakes,
With chatting leaves and munching snakes.

Acorns bounce from branch to ground,
Frogs add croaks to the merry sound.
Sunshine tickles every beam,
As feathered friends join in the dream.

Mice wear shoes of blades so green,
Dancing like they're in a scene.
With giggles echoing all around,
Nature's laughter knows no bounds.

The Epics of the Evergreen Elves

Elves in hats made out of pine,
Sip on dew, feeling so fine.
They plot adventures by moonlight,
With twinkling eyes, oh what a sight!

They race the wind, they chase the stars,
And stitch their cloaks with candy bars.
Frolicking under shadows tall,
Creating mischief, oh what a ball!

With every giggle, branches sway,
Telling secrets in a playful way.
Elves will dance till break of day,
In a forest brightly on display.

Shades of Saga in the Sylvan Realm

In a realm where shadows play,
Every leaf has jokes to say.
The tallest trunks nod with delight,
A messenger between day and night.

Pine cones giggle in the breeze,
Tickled by mischievous tease.
The pixies twirl with sprightly grace,
Spreading joy in every space.

From the roots to branches high,
Silly stories float on by.
Let's join the fun, let's sing along,
In the woodland where we belong!

Mirth of the Miniature Woods

In the shade where squirrels dance,
They plot and scheme in a nutty trance.
The owls wink with feathered grace,
As rabbits hop in a comical race.

In tiny hats, the mice convene,
Crafting plans for mischief unseen.
With twigs for swords and leaves for shields,
A battle rages in fun-filled fields.

Arboretum of Untold Stories

Whispers swirl in leafy seams,
As gnomes share their wildest dreams.
A crow cackles, holding a spell,
While hedgehogs giggle, oh what a hell!

The tree trunks laugh with ancient wit,
Telling tales that make the roots split.
With a thump and a bump, the acorns fall,
Each one a secret waiting to sprawl.

Heritages in the Hushed Grove

In twilight's glow, the shadows play,
As fireflies light up their silly ballet.
The frogs in tuxedos, oh how they croon,
While the breeze joins in with a funny tune.

Whimsical mushrooms wear silly hats,
While rabbits practice their acrobats.
The night unfolds with laughter in tow,
As owls hoot jokes to the leaves below.

Elixirs of Earthbound Fables

Bubbling potions beneath the bark,
Crafted by creatures, bright and stark.
A raccoon with goggles brews trouble and fun,
While spinning a tale under the golden sun.

The ants ride on ladybugs' backs,
In search of the stories that never relax.
With twinkling eyes and mischief galore,
They find the laughter that roots implore.

Evergreen Echoes: Celebrations of Growth

In the forest where giggles sprout,
Trees whisper tales of a playful rout.
Saplings dance with wind in glee,
Wagging branches, wild and free.

Squirrels throw acorn parties high,
With nuts as hats, they reach for the sky.
Laughter echoes, a merry sound,
As trunks do jiggle, roots rebound.

Birds wear ties made of leafy lace,
Thrilling chases in the green embrace.
While branches sway to the laugh track,
Their barky jokes will never lack.

Among the boughs, the critters play,
Tree frogs garden with jokes all day.
A festival of cheer, none can resist,
In this woody world, friendship twists.

Saga of the Sunlit Arboretum

In sunlit gaps, shadows prance,
Trees hold hands in a quirky dance.
Leaves that chuckle, branches sway,
Together they sing, a sunny ballet.

Photosynthetic jokes they crack,
While squirrels hop like they're on the track.
Nutty humor, woodpecker's cheer,
With laughter springing, all draw near.

Dancing trunks in autumn's breeze,
Accorns wearing capes with ease.
Each flick of foliage tells a tale,
As branches bend, they tip the scale.

Under the sun, in a leafy dome,
Roots weave a carpet, nature's home.
With barky banter, they celebrate,
The joy of green, they elevate.

Ballads of Beech and Oak

In a beech hat, an oak stands tall,
Telling jokes to the young and small.
Whispering winds, they spin a yarn,
While squirrels scamper, well-behaved on the lawn.

With acorns bouncing like playful cheers,
These tree pals laugh, year after year.
Gnarled branches twist in endless smiles,
A wooden party that stretches for miles.

Roots rumble softly, like a drum,
Sharing stories where laughter's from.
With every ring that adds to their age,
They pen funny lines upon nature's page.

So gather 'round for a leafy song,
As beech and oak prove laughter's strong.
In their sturdy shade, let's all partake,
In tales of joy that never break.

The Language of Lushness

With every leaf, a secret shared,
Tall trees giggle, nothing bared.
The brush of foliage, a cheeky wink,
Where nature's mischief makes us think.

Vines twist closely, in playful chat,
While branches swing like a big ol' cat.
A symphony of rustling green,
Their jokes are silly, wild, and keen.

Among bright flowers, laughter blooms,
Creeping vines host merry tunes.
The humor spreads like sunbeam rays,
Lushness speaks in funny ways.

So here we frolic, in a leafy spree,
Where greens converse, and glee is free.
Join the chorus, let joy increase,
In this lush world, we find release.

The Enchanted Woodland Symphony

In the forest, leaves do jig,
Squirrels dance, oh what a gig!
Frogs croak rhythm, bugs beat drums,
All join in, it really hums.

Breezes sway the branches high,
While the owls roll their big eyes.
The rabbits hop in tune so spry,
Blowing kisses to the sky.

Mushrooms tap their little toes,
As the pinecones shake with prose.
A symphony of nature's cheer,
Each note brings a giggle near.

So come and laugh beneath the sky,
Where trees perform as they comply.
In this quirky woodland space,
You'll find joy in every place.

Stories Intertwined in Green

Once a twig met a dandy leaf,
They shared tales, beyond belief.
A snail said, "Hold, don't go too fast!"
"I'll tell you secrets from the past!"

A raccoon chimed in, quite surprised,
"Did you hear about the owl's disguise?"
With each twist, a new plot grew,
In whispers soft, the stories flew.

Roots tangled in a curious dance,
While beetles plotted for romance.
The shadows giggled, crickets laughed,
A tapestry of fun they craft.

Beneath the branches, wild and free,
Stories weave a funny spree.
Each tree holds laughter, wisdom, too,
In their embrace, life feels brand new.

Soliloquy of the Swaying Boughs

Oh, how I stretch up to the sky,
Thoughts drift upwards, oh my, oh my!
With every gust, I bend and sway,
Chasing butterflies in playful play.

I ponder squirrels with nuts they stash,
And birds that swoop and dive in a flash.
Why do they chirp so early, though?
I'd like to know, do tell me, bro!

Every swishing branch has tales galore,
Of breezes, laughter, and so much more.
I talk to the stars, they wink and shine,
In this memory of branches divine.

So if you hear me whisper low,
It's just my secrets wanting to flow.
Join me, dear friend, for a giggle spree,
In this delightful dance of the trees.

Chronicles of the Verdant World

In a land where the daffodils play,
Grass tickles toes in a merry way.
Bees hold their dance with utmost glee,
Crafting stories beneath each tree.

Hopping bunnies with glittery eyes,
Chase shadows that look like pies.
While ants march on their tiny quest,
Searching for crumbs, they do their best.

Every leaf whispers of mishaps bright,
Like critters caught in a silly fight.
A hedgehog tripped, fell right on its back,
And laughed at the clouds for turning black.

Round and round, the stories spin,
Of furry friends in a playful din.
This verdant world, so wild and free,
Is bursting with joy and funny glee.

The Timeless Arbor Narratives

In a forest where squirrels play,
They practice gymnastics every day.
They flip and they twirl, oh what a sight,
While picking their acorns with sheer delight.

The trunks, they gossip, with branches that sway,
About the raccoon who lost his way.
He thought he was sneaky, oh what a tease,
But the owls just chuckled from high in the trees.

A woodpecker taps on a drum so grand,
Creating a concert, a woodland band.
The rabbits all dance in a hilarious line,
In a show that's so silly, it should be divine!

So here in the woods, the laughter does bloom,
With funny antics that cheer up the gloom.
Each tree is a storyteller, so wise and so spry,
In this quirky abode where the giggles never die.

Secrets of the Sylvan Shadows

Under leaves where the mischief thrives,
A chameleon juggles with squirrels and hives.
He changes his colors, a whimsical sight,
While the chipmunks laugh, oh what a delight!

The shadows hide tales of a cheeky old fox,
Who steals from the hens in mismatched socks.
He tiptoes away with a laugh and a wink,
And the trees all chuckle; they can't even think!

A band of raccoons wear hats made of leaves,
They pull magic tricks that no one believes.
With a swipe of a paw, they vanish from view,
Leaving only behind their favorite shoe!

The ferns whisper softly, with giggles on breeze,
As the creatures embark on their antics with ease.
In the shadiest nooks where the laughter will echo,
Life is a circus for every old and young fellow.

Whispers of the Woodland

In a meadow where daisies roll and spin,
A rabbit plays tug-of-war with a pin.
The turtle, so slow, just shakes his old head,
As the chase makes him dizzy, he'll nap instead.

The bushes are buzzing, a hive gone awry,
While a bee in a bowtie attempts to fly high.
But crash! He goes headfirst into some stew,
As the ladybugs giggle, they all shout, 'Boo-hoo!'

The trees lean in close, oh so full of mirth,
Sharing jokes about acorns and their worth.
One said, "I'm quite nutty!" and laughed with glee,
As the leaves rustle softly, 'Oh, can't you see?'

With each funny tale in the dappled shade,
The woodland becomes a grand masquerade.
As critters all prance, in this silliness sea,
Nature's companions are laughing with glee!

Canopy Chronicles

High above in the treetops so green,
A parrot spills secrets, oh what a scene.
He mimics the fox, with a sly little grin,
As the branches all wiggle, they join in the din.

The sunbeams race through the leaves on a dare,
While the butterflies gossip without a care.
With a flutter and flurry, they dance in the light,
Creating a ruckus, oh what a sight!

The squirrels organize a cheeky parade,
With acorns on floats that they cleverly made.
They throw nuts to the crowd, oh what a mess,
While the wise old owl just provides some finesse.

In the canopy high where the laughter will soar,
Nature's own circus is always in store.
With each twist and turn in this whimsical spree,
Every critter joins in for pure jubilee!

Shadows Among the Limbs

In the shade, squirrels dance around,
Chasing their tails without a sound.
They giggle and leap, or at least they try,
While the wise old owl just rolls an eye.

The branches sway, a comical show,
As birds argue loudly, putting on a flow.
They mimic each other with shrieks and squawks,
Creating a ruckus that never unlocks.

A raccoon slips down with a wash of hands,
Searching for snacks or forgotten bands.
As everyone scatters in humorous fright,
For the shadowy figure in the moonlight.

Laughter erupts like leaves in the breeze,
As nature's wild party is sure to please.
Hearts lift like branches, reaching the sky,
While shadows among the limbs wave goodbye.

Songs of the Rustic Canopy

Under the leaves, a chorus takes flight,
With branches as instruments, oh what a sight!
The rustle of leaves, like a drummer's beat,
Makes every critter dance on their feet.

A warbler croons, with a twinkle of cheer,
While a woodpecker tries to chime in near.
The laughter bubbles like a cool stream's flow,
As they harmonize here in the afternoon glow.

Chipmunks in hats tap their little toes,
As butterflies waltz, posing in rows.
The trees sway gently, joining the thrill,
Jiving with roots in a vibrant spill.

With each note echoing through vibrant air,
The canopy giggles, free without care.
Songs of the rustic, so playful and spry,
Leaves rustle softly, with laughter nearby.

Reveries of Root and Sky

Roots twist and turn, a comical sight,
Grabbing at rocks in a playful fight.
With every slip, the foliage breaks,
As mischief unfolds, oh what a ruckus it makes!

Up in the clouds, the branches do sway,
Tickling the sky in a whimsical play.
A crow takes a dive, with a wink and a wink,
While the branches giggle as they all rethink.

The rumbles below lead to chirps above,
As rabbits and foxes share a big shove.
They tumble and roll in nature's embrace,
While whispers of wind bring a grin to their face.

Reveries come, as shadows dance wild,
In the heart of the forest, nature's own child.
With laughter as light as the warm summer air,
Every root and branch shares a moment to share.

The Chronicles of Timbered Heights

Once upon a branch, there lived a fun crew,
With woodpeckers knocking, and crows yelling too.
The squirrel was king, with a crown made of acorns,
Claiming his throne while the fox filled with scorns.

The trees gathered 'round for a grand treelein,
As the breeze played piano, a natural sheen.
Chipmunks performed in a dazzling display,
Creating a show that stole night and day.

Tall tales were spun from trunks old and wise,
Where laughter echoed to the bright, open skies.
Timbered heights shook with hearty cheers,
As every critter bourbon-sized their fears.

The chronicles told of shadows and fun,
A forest so lively, uniting as one.
With giggles and whispers, the stories unfold,
Magic of nature, in ages untold.

Whispers of the Woodland Canopy

Squirrels chatter, what a show,
They plot and scheme while we all know.
Branches sway, a jig they start,
Nature's comedy, a work of art.

The owls wink with eyes so wide,
As chipmunks sneak off to hide.
Leaves perform a silly dance,
All around, there's giggles and prance.

Breezes tickle the boughs above,
Rustling secrets, whispers of love.
A raccoon rolls, too proud to fall,
Underneath it all, we laugh through it all.

With every rustle, a laugh we chase,
In this goofy, leafy place.
The canopy knows how to tease,
A laugh-filled realm, with such ease!

Secrets Beneath the Bark

Underneath, the critters squawk,
Mice are gossiping around the block.
Beneath the bark, a world so grand,
In tunnels of mischief, they make their stand.

Ants in line, a parade that's bold,
With tiny trumpets, their stories told.
Fungi giggle, mycelium fun,
What a party when day is done!

Worms are the jesters, spinning tales,
Of leaf treks and snowy gales.
Under the surface, laughter flies,
As chirps and peeps fill the skies.

Secrets bubble, a hidden cheer,
Nature's jesters always near.
In the earth, jokes spin and wriggle,
A surprise awaits with every giggle!

The Dance of Leaf and Branch

Leaves are twirling, a breezy ballet,
While branches chuckle, come join the play.
Swaying low with a goofy style,
Each gust of wind brings a cheeky smile.

The twiggy tap dance, stomp and prance,
Nature holds its joyful chance.
With every shake, the laughter pops,
As acorns tumble and twigs do hops.

Sunshine glimmers on this stage,
Forest giggles, can't help but engage.
Dancing around, all creatures cheer,
In synchronized antics, we draw near.

The branches bow, a comic grace,
In this vibrant, leafy space.
Every rustling note sings a laugh,
The dance goes on, nature's own craft!

Echoes of the Ancient Grove

In the grove where whispers play,
Ancient trees tell tales all day.
Barking at jokes from long ago,
Their laughter echoes, a funny flow.

Twisted trunks with grins so wide,
Each knot holds stories they can't hide.
Their rings count laughs, not just the years,
As critters join in with squeaky cheers.

The breeze joins in, a chuckling friend,
With every since, the giggles blend.
As shadows dance on the forest floor,
Laughter lingers, inviting more.

Mushrooms pop up, bright with mirth,
In this ancient realm of merry birth.
The echoes drift like tales of old,
In this grove, laughter is uncontrolled!

The Feel of Forest Floor Tales

In shadows deep where critters play,
A squirrel slips, then rolls away.
He clutches nuts with wobbly flair,
While mushrooms giggle, unaware.

The rabbits hop in silly dance,
They trip on roots, but take a chance.
With floppy ears and whiskers twitch,
They flee from leaves, which seem to glitch.

A fox stands tall with mischief grins,
He tells tall tales with crafty spins.
But all the trees just shake their heads,
While owls remark on hatter's threads.

And so the forest hums along,
With tales of whimsy, bright and strong.
As beetles roll like velvet balls,
Their laughter echoes through the halls.

Timelessness Beneath the Terrain

Under roots the secrets lie,
Where ants hold court and steal the pie.
The mushrooms wear their hats with pride,
And plan a dance, though shy inside.

The snail moves slow, a comical feat,
While silly bugs sneak quick to eat.
With tiny trumpets they parade,
Amongst the grass, in laughter played.

The earthworms wiggle, oh so sly,
They scoff at rocks that stand nearby.
As bunnies munch on dandelion,
They scheme for snacks, their heads aligned.

Underneath, the tales unfold,
With giggles shared, and dreams retold.
For every creature has its part,
In this vast world, a leafy art.

The Lore of Leaf and Limb

The branches wave like silly arms,
In breezes strong, they share their charms.
They play a game of peek-a-boo,
With sun rays shining right on cue.

The leaves gossip in a soft sound,
While falling softly to the ground.
They whirl and twirl, a colorful spree,
As squirrels plot their jolly glee.

A raccoon grins with sticky paws,
While fruit spills out from hidden drawers.
He dances round in playful grace,
While shadows swish, they leave no trace.

In branches thick, a nest of jokes,
Where sparrows sing and tease the folks.
The forest chuckles, wild and free,
In a jest that flows like a carefree sea.

Canopies of Captivating Itineraries

Above the ground, a rooftop maze,
Where squirrels plot their jumpy ways.
They scurry high and dive down low,
In playful leaps, just for show.

A wily crow with tricks up sleeve,
Swoops down low to join the weave.
With flapping wings, a comic flight,
He toots a tune, much to delight.

The branches creak in laughter's gain,
As creatures dance through sun and rain.
They swap their stories on a breeze,
With endless joy among the trees.

In canopies, where fun does thrive,
The spirit of the wild comes alive.
And all beneath the leafy scenes,
A world of humor, swift and keen.

Grove Guardians: Tales Unseen

In the glade where shadows creep,
Squirrels plot their grand leap.
A raccoon dons a leafy hat,
Declaring himself the king of that!

With acorns stacked like tiny pies,
The wise old owl hoots out his lies.
He claims he knows the best hot springs,
But only bathes in puddles, poor thing!

A hedgehog joins the dance, oh so bold,
Twirling 'round, if you can behold.
But trips on roots, with a clumsy roll,
The grove erupts in laughter's stroll!

So here they gather, creatures spry,
With giggles echoing 'neath the sky.
Where the unseen tales twist and turn,
And laughter flares, as hearts all yearn.

Sprouts of Solitude

In a quiet nook, a rabbit sings,
Alone but proud, with imaginary wings.
He hosts a party for ants and flies,
With tiny cakes that make them sighs.

A cactus dreams of being a tree,
Complains of not having any leaves to be.
While lonely rootworms dance in sand,
Wishing to twirl with a stem so grand.

A lonesome breeze starts to hum a tune,
Tickling branches beneath the moon.
A dandelion joins, with fluff on its head,
Celebrating life, with joy instead!

Together they laugh at their quirky plight,
In solitude's arms, they find delight.
For in this grove, each tale unfurls,
As sprouts of solitude create their whirls.

Memories of the Mighty Canopy

Once a squirrel stole a peanut prize,
But forgot where it hid, much to his surprise.
Now he listens to mushrooms tell tales,
Of treasures that grow in roots and trails.

A wise slug slides slow, with wisdom grand,
Telling secrets, as time's gentle hand.
His tales of rain and sun are a treat,
As everyone gathers for this slug-shaped seat.

The wind whispers stories, tall and spry,
Of leaves that giggle, and branches that fly.
Each rustling laugh fills the air with glee,
Reminiscing moments yet to be.

In the hollow of wood, a bear once danced,
While bats above twinkled, entranced.
These memories blend in a vibrant spree,
Of laughter echoing through the mighty spree!

A Tapestry of Timber Tales

In a forest where shadows weave,
A beaver swims, wearing leaves.
He claims to be the finest chef,
But just makes soup from twigs, oh, the clef!

A crow caws out with sass and flair,
As trees prepare their own sweet fair.
With berries spritzed and nuts on strings,
They put on ponchos, their festival brings!

A badger winks, a trickster true,
Plants potato chips for a furry crew.
A feast of laughter, a playful spree,
In this woven realm of timber glee!

As night falls gently, the tales ignite,
With fireflies dancing, oh what a sight!
A tapestry formed by the night's embrace,
Where funny stories find their place.

Fables of the Forest

In the woods, where giggles sprout,
Squirrels chatter, running about.
Rabbits hop in silly shoes,
Trading tales of silly snooze.

Foxes dance in leafy hats,
Chasing shadows, flirting with rats.
A bear who thinks he's quite a star,
Playing jazz on an old guitar.

The owls hoot in such delight,
Cracking jokes in the moonlight.
Every branch has laughter stored,
In this place, joy is adored.

Under skies with colors bright,
Every creature shares a light.
For in this world that's full of glee,
Life's a jest, so come and see!

Secrets Beneath the Bark

Beneath the bark, a gnome resides,
He tells tall tales, with great strides.
A ladybug wearing a tiny crown,
Claims she's the queen of this small town.

The ants march in a funny line,
Holding hands, feeling so fine.
While the fireflies start a show,
In flickering lights of toe-to-toe.

A worm with glasses reads a book,
On how to dance with a silly look.
The trees all chuckle as they sway,
Listening to this strange cabaret.

All these secrets, just for you,
In whispers from the morning dew.
Silly tunes from trunks that sway,
What fun and games they have each day!

The Saga of Silent Sentinels

In the quiet glen, tall friends stand,
Guarding secrets of the land.
A parrot with a twinkle in his eye,
Claims to know just how to fly.

With every breeze, they sway and dance,
Bark-clad jesters, taking a chance.
Raccoons juggling acorns with glee,
While frogs croak tunes for all to see.

Beneath the shade, the laughter roars,
Echoing on forgotten shores.
Every knot and twist reveals,
A charming tale that laughter steals.

The sentinels share their silly tales,
Of mischief done in nature's gales.
So, listen close, for stories wheat,
In this forest, life is sweet!

Echoes in the Grove

In the grove where giggles bloom,
Everything dispels the gloom.
A chipmunk with a curious stare,
Wears a hat and says, "Life's a fair!"

The trees whisper jokes to each other,
Singing tales of how they smother.
With roots that tickle and branches that tease,
Planting joy in the rushing breeze.

With every rustle, life unfolds,
In playful whispers, and tales retold.
The bushy tails of glee parade,
Beneath the sun's warm serenade.

So step right up to join the fun,
In the grove, where laughter's spun.
Echoes ring through leaf and bark,
Where every heart can leave a mark!

Swaying in Sylvan Dreams

In the glade where the squirrels play,
A raccoon steals lunch from the buffet.
Branching out with a cheeky grin,
Each nut's a prize he's destined to win.

With acorns tumbling like comets bright,
A beaver debates if they're worth the bite.
The woodpecker laughs, his drill on the scene,
Knocking on wood like a drummer keen.

When the wind whispers tales of delight,
A snail races past, giving quite a fright.
Who knew speed could be found in a shell?
Yet here in the woods, it's a laugh to tell!

As branches wiggle with mirth in the air,
The shadows waltz with a light-hearted flair.
Nature's a stage, and we're all in tune,
With giggles and grins beneath the bright moon!

Fables of the Hidden Forest

A wise old owl hoots at the moon,
"Who's there?" asks a dogwood, far too soon.
A squirrel on a branch shouts, "Turn off that light!
It's way past our bedtime; let's sleep tonight!"

The porcupine juggles his quills with great ease,
While beetles play tag like they've caught a breeze.
A butterfly twirls and trips on a leaf,
Stumbling and laughing—nature's own chief!

"Why do you wear those prickly cute bragging rights?"
The rabbit hops over and lounges in sights.
"Because it's a shield," quipped the porcupine proud,
"To keep my best moves from crowds too loud!"

A fox throws a party, leaves flutter and sway,
With dances and prancing, they celebrate play.
The trees clap their hands, all in good cheer,
As laughter rings out, filling the clear!

Unfurled Feathers of the Green Realm

A parrot squawks jokes from high in the oak,
Leaving all critters in stitches, a joke poke.
The finches join in, harmonious shrills,
With punchlines popping like daffodil pills.

A turtle groans slow, but with a sly wink,
As the frogs croak sonnets by the cool drink.
"Leap, leap, the world is a jolly stage!"
Oh, if only stories were penned on each page!

Leprechaun lizards flaunt fortune so grand,
Trading treasures for tales across the woodland.
They giggle and dance, those sprightly little things,
As butterflies flutter with laughter on wings.

The green realm is rich with joy that abounds,
Where every old joke is spun round and round.
Nature's whimsy hides clever delights,
In the playful rustle of leaves through the nights!

Tales from the Trunk's Embrace

Beneath a stout trunk, the critters convene,
Sharing tall tales of the sights they have seen.
The badger boasts boldly of travels afar,
While the porcupine dreams of a ride in a car.

Fancy a picnic? The hedgehogs all sing,
With strawberries plump, and sweet scones to bring.
A daring old crow eyes the feast from the sky,
"Don't mind me, friends, just a bird passing by!"

The mouse tells a story of cheese-shaped delight,
While folks start to giggle at shadows of night.
A chubby old raccoon, all socks on his feet,
Claims the cake is best when it's served with a beat!

When stars start to twinkle, the scene gets quite bright,
As the creatures all dance with insatiable might.
With laughter and whimsy, they twirl and embrace,
All gathered together, the trunk is their place!

Saga of the Symphony of Sap

In a forest where sap sings,
A chorus of squirrels brings flings.
Chirping with joy, they leap and bound,
In rhythm with bushes they frolic around.

Bumbles of bees crash with flair,
What are they thinking? Do they care?
Bouncing on branches, a comedic sight,
As they buzz around in dizzy delight.

With a plucky raccoon on a ukelele,
Strumming tunes that are jazzy and jelly.
Dancing with leaves in a whimsical feast,
His furry friends join in, at least!

A chorus of laughter fills the air,
Nature's own circus, beyond compare.
Widget the owl hoots from high,
"Keep it down, you rascals, or I might just cry!"

Arboreal Anecdotes

Once a chipmunk wore a hat quite grand,
With feathers plucked from a roaming band.
Sauntering proud, he thought he'd impress,
But tripped on a twig and made a big mess.

A wise old oak chuckled from afar,
"Fashion is folly, but you're a star!"
With squirrels in stiches, they all took glee,
Who knew that such fashion was bound to be free?

Tales of raccoons who swiped a snack,
Using their paws, they formed a small pack.
But the pie they pilfered rolled down the hill,
Their howls of dismay were such a thrill!

The trees whispered secrets as laughter spread,
Echoing joys from the fun they wed.
Among the branches, their stories twirled,
In the spicy wind, their antics unfurled.

Legends Carved in Bark

A tale of a beaver with dreams so bold,
He thought he could build a fortress of gold.
But logs piled high became absurd,
"Why is it swaying?" Our hero once heard!

With every chip and every bite,
He crafted a mess in the shimmering light.
His buddies all snickered, "You've built a boat!"
But he just waved back, "Enjoy the float!"

A parrot who squawked of big jungle fame,
Declared he could beat any flamingo's game.
But while aiming for elegance, he fell on a vine,
And ended up tangled, looking quite fine!

So for legends of laughter wrapped up in bark,
Embrace the fun; make your own mark.
For nature is witty, a riotous spree,
In tales of the wood, all are quite free!

Wind's Story within the Foliage

The wind whispers gossip to branches above,
Tickling the leaves with a tender shove.
"Did you hear, the owl sings off key?
His last attempt was a sight to see!"

Swaying and chuckling, the foliage sways,
Capturing tales of the oddest of days.
Johnny the crow, quite the jokester indeed,
"Who thought I'd be funny?" was his proud need.

A gust of mischief, it tickles the pine,
"Grab the acorns, we'll toast with the wine!"
But acorns are slippery, they roll and they skitter,
"Forget the feast, don't let the wind flitter!"

So round and around, the stories would weave,
From arching old oaks to the slick autumn leaves.
In the laughter of nature, all creatures agree,
It's all in good fun amongst roots, wild and free!

The Heartbeat of the Wildwood

In the forest where laughter roams,
Squirrels hold meetings in tiny homes.
With acorn hats, they dance and enjoy,
Chasing their shadows, oh what a ploy!

The owls wear glasses, quite a sight,
Reading the stars every single night.
Rabbits with pragmatism, hopping on cue,
Argue with hedgehogs, 'Is grass really blue?'

A bear with a bowtie, looking so neat,
Wants to join in on the festive beat.
Bumblebees buzzing in rhythmic delight,
Holding a concert till early twilight.

With every giggle and rustle around,
Joy paints the air, with laughter it's crowned.
In wildwood's heart, where mischief ignites,
The pulse of the forest, a cacophony of sights!

Stories Woven in Twigs

A spider spins tales in a silken chair,
An ant drops in with nibbles to share.
They plot a grand heist of the cookie jar,
While a crow caws loudly, 'I'm the star!'

Chirp of the crickets, a slapstick scene,
With fireflies glowing in hues of green.
They dance to the rhythm of a bouncing toad,
Throwing a giggle storm off the road.

Twigs play the strings for a woodland band,
Frogs croak the tune while they take a stand.
'Can you hear us?' the berries shout with glee,
Find out the truth when they spill the tea!

As the sun sets down, with laughter in tow,
The stories unfold, and oh how they flow!
In a canopy maze, where fun intertwines,
Mirth is the secret, in whispers it chimes.

Tales from the Boughs

Under the boughs where the giggles reside,
A woodpecker drums, with glee as his guide.
Raccoons point and laugh at the squirrel's new dare,
As they sit in a circle, nuts everywhere!

The owls play poker beneath the moonlight,
Betting on beetles, oh what a sight!
Wombats pull pranks, while trees sway and sway,
'This place is a riot!' the cedars would say.

A parrot pops by just to share some zest,
Telling tall tales, putting wit to the test.
The whispering wind joins in with a shout,
'Gather 'round creatures; let's all take a route!'

With each turn of a leaf, the fun drifts and sways,
Where laughter is nestled in sunbeam rays.
So come join the chorus, let joy find its way,
In the grand old oaks where the wild things play!

In the Embrace of the Evergreens

Beneath the evergreens, a party ensues,
Where critters gather to exchange silly news.
A hedgehog with glasses sips elderberry tea,
Humming a tune, oh so brilliantly!

The chipmunks compete in a nutty relay,
Racing through branches, come join the display!
Swooping down swiftly, the jay cracks a joke,
'Last one to the pond is a silly old bloke!'

The pines are amused by the antics so bright,
Whispering secrets in the cool moonlight.
While bunnies spin tales of heroic demands,
'The garden is ours, let's take a few stands!'

A chorus of chuckles rings out through the wood,
Each creature conspiring just as they should.
With mirth in the air and joy in their hearts,
They dance and they twirl till the daylight departs!

Epiphanies in Dappled Light

Beneath the rays of the sun's warm art,
Squirrels plot mischief, a bushy-tailed start.
They chatter and dance with acorn dreams,
As shadows play games, or so it seems.

The branches giggle in a feathery sway,
While leaves share secrets of the cheeky jay.
A curious worm joins the leafy fun,
Saying, "Life underground can't hurt, just run!"

A raccoon, with style, struts on a limb,
Wearing a mask, but he doesn't look prim.
He steals a bird's snack, then puffs out his chest,
Quipping, "I'm the bandit! Just call me the best!"

In this bright haven, where laughter flows,
Nature's kookiness constantly shows.
Each creature's a player in life's little play,
Dancing in sunlight, come join the fray!

Whispers Among the Old Growth

In the heart of the woods, the wise trees conspire,
With stories of mischief that never seem dire.
A beetle in armor declares he's a knight,
While shadows of owls take wing in delight.

"Who knew the ferns would host such a show?"
Crickets dress up, but they don't want to grow.
They chirp out a tune with a silly refrain,
As fireflies twinkle, their spirits insane.

An ancient old pine fumbles at jokes,
Every knot in his bark holds high, hearty pokes.
The wisdom he shares, with a chuckle and grin,
Makes laughter erupt from the roots to the fin.

Thus the canopy smiles with stories galore,
Each rustling leaf a giggle, a roar.
Navigating the laughter, let's take a chance,
Amongst the old growth, come join the dance!

The Odyssey of the Arbor Life

A tiny acorn dreams of the sky,
"Before sunrises, I want to fly!"
But first, a worm gives him wise, soft advice,
"Stay grounded, little one, be patient; it's nice."

As seasons roll by, through rain and through sun,
Our acorn takes root, both sturdy and fun.
With limbs that reach high and whispers so true,
"Hey bird, try the shade; it's the best with a view!"

A squirrel swings by, with stories to share,
"Join me for jesting, there's fruit in the air!
Let's fashion a feast with a nutty embrace,
Where all furry friends can find a warm place."

So the branches all chuckle, and the leaves dance along,
As an orchestra plays nature's delightful song.
An odyssey blooms where the laughter runs free,
In the splendid embrace of the grand O-a-k tree!

Parables from the Gnarled Woods

In gnarled old woods where the stories are spun,
A raccoon declares, "I'm the funniest one!"
With each twist and turn of a crooked design,
Each crevice and knot has a tale that's divine.

A wise old owl hoots from a perch up so high,
"Tales of big blunders and silly goodbye.
When a fox tried to dance in a toadstool parade,
He tripped on his tail and the whole thing just swayed!"

Beneath the green canopy, laughter does gleam,
Where stories unfold like a whimsical dream.
A rabbit recounts tales of hats and of shoes,
Saying, "It's okay if you're making the snooze!"

From roots down below to branches that wave,
The parables shine, and the creatures all rave.
For in gnarled old woods, with laughter in air,
Life is a party; so come if you dare!

Murmurs of the Verdant Realm

In the jungle, a squirrel sings,
Hiding acorns with silly flings.
Parrots squawk, their colors bold,
Trading gossip, secrets told.

The banyan tree starts to sway,
Tickling the bees in their busy play.
Leaves whisper jokes, quite absurd,
While butterflies chuckle, undeterred.

A chameleon wears a bright bow tie,
Dancing around, oh my, oh my!
Branches chuckle, roots giggle low,
In this green realm, laughter will flow.

When the sun dips low and shadows prance,
Lizards join in a silly dance.
The forest rumbles, a playful scene,
Nature's humor, evergreen and keen.

Threads of Flora and Fauna

A mischievous mouse in a thicket creeps,
Knitting with grass, while a raccoon peeks.
The daisies gossip, petals in whirl,
As sunflowers spin, giving a twirl.

A dandelion puff, a cozy hat,
On a curious cat where it softly sat.
Worms form a band in their muddy domain,
Singing sweet tunes in a wormy refrain.

Tadpoles in puddles, diving with cheer,
Splashing in water, spreading their fear.
The lilies laugh, the frogs leap high,
Oh what a circus beneath the sky!

With each flutter, each rustle, each fun-filled quirk,
Life weaves its magic, where laughter does lurk.
In this playful patch of green delight,
Nature's a jester, both day and night.

Legends Carved in Bark

Once upon a time, a squirrel so sly,
Challenged the owl to give it a try.
With nut in its paw, it claimed it could fly,
And leapt from a branch with a comical cry.

An ancient oak chuckles, holding the tale,
Of the frog that thought it could sing like a whale.
The wind carries echoes of laughter and cheer,
As leaves dance around to the stories they hear.

Feathers and fur join the delightful din,
While tree trunks giggle at where to begin.
Each bark-etched story, a quirky delight,
Turns forest whispers into magical night.

So gather 'round roots to listen and dream,
For nature's a bard with a mischievous beam.
In the shadows of giants, the legends will flow,
Where whispers of humor and wonder do grow.

Twilight among the Twigs

When dusk falls softly, the crickets start,
A raccoon juggles, with skill and art.
Fireflies twinkle like stars in disguise,
As the trees wear night's sparkles with sighs.

A wise old owl hoots old jokes with glee,
While ants plan a party beneath the pine tree.
Mice bring the snacks, a banquet so grand,
While the wind strums a tune, a soft, breezy band.

Bats swoop and dive, a comical sight,
Flapping their wings in pure, silly flight.
The moon winks down at this jovial scene,
Nature's night carnival, merry and keen.

So raise a twig toast to the dusk and the play,
For laughter and joy light the end of the day.
In the heart of the woods, where shadows will prance,
Every creature will join in this delightful dance.

Growth Rings of Time

In circles we grow, round and round,
With stories untold, in layers we're found.
Each year we add, a ring of our quest,
A party of time, in nature's fest!

Beneath the sun's rays, we dance in delight,
Sharing our secrets, beneath the moonlight.
With squirrels and birds, we swing with glee,
In this great big park, oh, just let us be!

We laugh at the winds, as they tickle our tips,
While fawns play tag, with their slippery slips.
Our branches wave high, like they're doing a jig,
With the pine cones joining in, what a big gig!

So cheers to the moments, we stretch and we sway,
As laughter and joy paint the green display.
For every ring tells a tale so divine,
In the loop of our lives, everything's fine!

Barkskins and Branchbound Secrets

Under the bark, oh what a mix!
Whispers of secrets, and leafy tricks.
Gossip in shadows, the sunlight peeks,
Tickling the branches with playful squeaks.

Between the knuckles, a giggle goes loud,
The owls hoot back, they've gathered a crowd.
While fungi perform their moldy ballet,
The sunbeams laugh, 'Come join the play!'

A hedgehog rolls by, in search of a prize,
'What's under this bush?' with curious eyes.
We chuckle and sigh at the mess he makes,
As twigs twist and turn, oh the fun it takes!

So if you venture where the bark is thick,
Listen real close for a chirp or a click.
For laughter and joy is what rules this place,
In a world full of wonders, just give it a chase!

Conversations in the Canopy Above

In high places where we sway,
Conversations bounce in a leafy ballet.
With chipmunks chattering and robins on cue,
Every branch holds a tale, fresh and new.

The breeze whispers jokes, a subtle tease,
As acorns drop down with grace, if you please.
We chuckle together, as shadows dance by,
Hiding our giggles, just you and I.

The sun winks at us through the green lace,
While butterflies flutter, a colorful race.
With laughter we sing, a raucous delight,
A canopy choir under stars so bright.

So lift up your gaze, let the stories unfold,
Of laughter and joy that never grows old.
For up in the heights, life's humor is clear,
In the leaves intertwined, we're always sincere!

The Heartbeat of the Forest Floor

Down in the earth, a rumble and roll,
Where mischievous critters give heartbeats a goal.
The roots wiggle and giggle in the soil they call home,
Telling tall tales, wherever they roam.

With worms in a wiggle, they dance underground,
A funky little beat that vibrates all around.
While mushrooms pop up for an underground show,
With laughter and joy, they put on a glow!

Beetles boast loudly of treasures they've found,
As ants have a meeting to discuss the ground.
With roots doing jazz, oh what a sight,
The forest floor's a party, full of delight!

So drop down low, just hear the fun thrive,
Feel the pulse of the earth, so lively and live.
For in every heartbeat, a tale does unfold,
In the depths of the forest, watch stories be told!

The Dance of Leaf and Limb

In the breeze, they shimmy and sway,
Branches twirl, like they're having a play.
Leaves chuckle as they flutter about,
Nature's own dancers, there's never a doubt.

Pine cones bounce, like clumsy old folks,
Twirling their canes, cracking jokes that evoke.
The oak takes a spin, with a flourish and spin,
Even the saplings join in, cheeky grins.

A worm on a branch does a wiggly twist,
"Come join the fun!" all the saplings insist.
But the heavy old willow shakes off its leaves,
Grumbling and mumbling, "These follies are thieves!"

Yet laughter rings high, as the fronds sway carefree,
In a dazzling display, oh what a sight to see!
Every knot and every bough, they join in the mirth,
In the woodland ballet, there's joy on the earth.

Shadows of the Ancient Stalks

Beneath the tall giants, shadows play free,
Spinning in circles, like a striped bee.
Roots with a chuckle, wiggle and writhe,
Making shapes funny, keeping sprigs alive.

"Hey there, good buddy!" says a stout old bark,
"I'll race you to sunset, just meet me at dark!"
And the roots, with a laughter, line up for the chase,
A root-race extravaganza, what a beautiful place!

Every time they fall, they land with a thud,
It's a playground of timber, a soft earthy mud.
The beetles and bugs cheer, they shout with delight,
As shadows stretch tall, in the warm afternoon light.

So if you find yourself, in a moment of glee,
Join the ancient shadows, come dance with the tree!
In the laughter of roots and boughs, just you wait,
The quirks of the forest are simply first-rate!

Legends of the Timbered Realm

In a place where the branches brush the sky,
Lies a kingdom where snails go zooming by.
Legends tell tales of a squirrel dressed fine,
Who threw the best parties on top of a pine.

With acorn confetti and berries galore,
The critters all gather, they stomp and they roar.
They whistle and giggle, and dance on the leaves,
A festivity brewing, oh what a tease!

The fox plays the flute made of hollowed-out bark,
While raccoons serve snacks in the light after dark.
The lessons of laughter echo high in the trees,
As the wise old owl hoots, "Just enjoy, if you please!"

So when you tread lightly on paths made of dreams,
Remember the laughter, the joys, and the beams.
This timbered realm's spirit will bring you a smile,
Join in on the legend, it's always worthwhile!

Voices from the Verdant Heights

Up in the treetops, where the sun loves to peek,
Voices are chatting, and they plot and they squeak.
"Have you seen that robin, he sings quite absurd!"
"Oh yes, he thinks he's the best in the herd!"

The leaves share a secret, they rustle with glee,
About the squirrel who thought he could fly from a tree.
With a leap and a flump, he descended with flair,
"I meant to do that!" he smirked, in midair!

The frogs on the lilies laugh ribbits of love,
While the ants throw a party in the grass below,
Everyone joins in, making jests without fear,
These voices of nature are music to hear!

So if you wander high where the branches align,
Listen to the echoes, their laughter divine.
In the verdant heights, with each branch and each vine,
The forests are buzzing, where funny rules shine!

Chronicles of the Bark-bound Beings

In the hollow of a limb, they shout,
With laughter loud, they twist about.
Jumpy squirrels dance on branches high,
While the old owl hoots a silly cry.

Whispering winds play tag with leaves,
Each flap and flutter, no one believes.
Down falls a nut, a plop and a tumble,
As giggles erupt in the boughs of the jumble.

Acorns roll far in a playful race,
While chipmunks dive into their warm space.
With each rustle, a joke's in the air,
The trunks and limbs share secrets they dare.

Frogs croak in tune with the branches' sway,
Oh, the antics of those who play all day!
As shadows stretch long in the golden light,
Bark-bound beings pull pranks all night!

Song of the Swaying Saplings

Little sprigs dance in a fanciful tune,
Bending and swaying beneath the warm moon.
They giggle and chatter with breezy delight,
In the flicker of stars, they frolic all night.

Curious critters peek from the green,
What silliness, they've surely keen!
Shaking their leaves, the saplings call,
To join in the fun, "Come one, come all!"

Silly shadows play hide and seek,
The giggling gang gets lost in a peek.
With laughter they tumble, so sprightly and free,
In the waltz of the winds, there's joy you can see.

With roots in a twist and futures bright,
They gather together and dance with delight.
As dew drops sparkle before the sun's rise,
The saplings will sing, bringing smiles and surprise!

Tales from the Twisted Trunks

In a wood where the trunks are goofy and bold,
They trade little tales that are funny and old.
Bark wrapped in knots, they chuckle and cheer,
Turning round trees, have a drink—grab a beer!

One trunk wears a hat made of twig and leaves,
Says it's true style, "No one believes!"
The others all snicker, their laughter will ring,
As mossy companions join in sing-spring!

Twirled and tangled in a playful array,
They swap silly secrets in their own way.
With branches a-wobble, they share all their woes,
While the frogs on their knuckles hop high in rows.

As shadows grow long, and the stars start to gleam,
Twisted trunks gather, a peculiar team.
"Tell one more tale before we sleep tight!"
They erupt with giggles, oh, what a night!

Blooming Mysteries in the Breeze

Petals fall gently, the blooms start to sway,
Whispering stories of the bright spring day.
A flower trips over its own vibrant hue,
And giggles erupt as soft petals construe.

In the laughter of blooms, a riddle unfolds,
As the bee hums sweet tales that nature beholds.
"Why did the blossom paint itself green?"
"Because it was jealous, or so it was seen!"

The sunshine giggles as the colors collide,
Every blossom a friend, they won't run and hide.
Breezes join in with a whirling caper,
As seeds set free dance in the paper.

Buds whisper secrets in the soft summer air,
Trading their stories without any care.
With each bloom and breeze, a new joke is spun,
In the garden of giggles, oh, what fun has begun!

The Lifeblood of the Rooted Kingdom

In a kingdom of roots and knee-high grass,
The critters all gather, oh what a class!
Squirrels in helmets, a rallying sight,
Racing to acorns, with all of their might.

The bunnies in boots prance all around,
Chasing after shadows, they're barely found.
With giggles and hiccups, they jump and they play,
While birds in fine suits lead the grand ballet.

The toads in their ties croak jokes in the night,
As fireflies twinkle with laughter and light.
Tree trunks are stages for all to perform,
In this jolly realm where the odd is the norm.

So here in this realm, let all voices rise,
With each little giggle, the forest complies.
For every good friend, no matter how small,
In this rooted domain, there's room for us all.

Bindings of the Green Guardians

Green guardians gather all round the old oak,
With whispers of wisdom and laughter's bespoke.
A snail wearing glasses reads us a tale,
Of frogs and their dances, and how they set sail.

Amidst the thick vines, a raccoon plays drums,
While owls on the sidelines all hoot to the hums.
A sloth in a lab coat checks every beat,
Scouting for rhythm on paws and on feet.

The bushes now bob, swaying side to side,
As critters assemble with joy and with pride.
With every small twist and a funny little laugh,
The trees hug them close, forming a safe path.

And still every rustle, each sigh from the leaves,
Is filled with the cheer that the forest believes.
In the bindings they share, both giggles and glee,
They weave up a wonder that's truly carefree.

Whimsy in the Willow's Whisper

The willow leans low, its whispers so sly,
Tickling the tigers as they stroll by.
"Why don't you join us for tea in the shade?
With biscuits and giggles, the forest's parade!"

A chipmunk in tux, with a bowl of fine treats,
Serves berries and nuts to all the gnarled feet.
With laughter like bubbles, the rabbits all share,
Tales of their stunts in mid-air, filled with flair.

The frogs croak a chorus, while crickets compose,
As fireflies dance, in the moonlight, they pose.
The scene sparkles bright with a gleeful delight,
A carnival hidden in the stillness of night.

So hush now and listen, hear whimsy unwind,
In whispers of willows, new laughter we find.
In this funny old grove where fantasies dwell,
Each tale brings us closer, as we ring the bell.

Reflections Among the Boughs

Beneath the broad branches, reflections abound,
Where mirrors of humor and joy can be found.
A parrot in puns, with a flair for the jest,
Keeps teasing the turtles, who ponder their quest.

They dance on the leaves with a silly old step,
As branches above them sway and then prep.
With giggles and nudges, they share their sweet cheer,
In a world where the odd doesn't seem so severe.

The echoes of laughter, a sweet serenade,
While shadows play tag in the light of the glade.
The wise old raccoon shares tales of the past,
As squirrels spin yarns that go by way too fast.

So come join the fun, swing low and swing high,
In the canopy's cover, let your spirit fly.
In refractions of glee, where who knows what's true,
Each chuckle unravels life's quirky debut.

The Poetry of Petrichor Amongst the Branches

Raindrops dance on leaves so green,
A slippery stage, a playful scene.
Squirrels slip and tumble down,
In their acorn jackets, a funny crown.

Wind whispers jokes to trunks so stout,
While branches sway, they twist about.
A woodpecker drums a silly beat,
As critters laugh from their leafy seat.

Clouds play peek-a-boo with the sun,
Nature's games are never done.
Each raindrop splashes, a giggling splash,
Under the canopy, where we all dash.

And as the puddles start to gleam,
The trees conspire, plotting a scheme.
To catch us laughing, dancing with glee,
In this merry forest, wild and free.

Fragments of a Leafy Legend

Once a leaf tried to tell a tale,
About a sprout, so small and frail.
With a whisper, it drifted down,
To crown a worm with a leafy crown.

The squirrel said with a cheeky grin,
"You think you're wise, but where've you been?"
Amidst the branches, echoes of fun,
A chorus of laughter, nature's pun.

A fluttering leaf with a wild dance,
Challenged the wind to a silly chance.
They twirled and spun in cheerful glee,
A spectacle for all, come watch and see!

In the tales of bark and stories untold,
Lies a legend wacky yet bold.
Nature chuckles beneath the skies,
With every twist and every surprise!

The Wisdom of Weathered Wood

Upon a bench of weathered grain,
Sits an old gnome with a wise refrain.
"Listen close," says he with a wink,
"The trees have secrets, so just think!"

"Once a twig said, 'I'm strong and grand,'
But winds of fate had other plans at hand.
So now I stand all twisted and bent,
But wise is the tree that once was content!"

The laughter rings with a bark so deep,
While creatures gather, secrets they keep.
In knots and grooves, adventures unfold,
Of fungi fungi and treasures untold.

With each squirrel's leap and scamper so quick,
The old gnome chuckles, giving a flick.
"Embrace your wobbles," he'll always say,
"For the heart of the forest lives in play!"

Murmurs of the Mossy Canopy

Beneath the green, the whispers grow,
Mossy tales that steal the show.
A raccoon hides with a twinkling eye,
In the shade where secrets sigh.

Toads croak jokes with a humorous twist,
While dragonflies add to the mist.
The trees nod along, their roots in the game,
As they giggle with leaves, never the same.

"Who's the jester up in the limb?"
Said a barky friend, on a playful whim.
From the canopy, echoes of cheer,
As nature chuckles, always near.

So if you wander in this wonderland,
Remember to pause, give laughter a hand.
For in the hush of the leafy wall,
The forest has jokes for one and all!

www.ingramcontent.com/pod-product-compliance
Lightning Source LLC
Chambersburg PA
CBHW051651160426
43209CB00004B/876